Holding Magnetic Conversations

Learn to Be a Master Communicator in Just Hours

By W. James Dennis

Sign-up now for free news, reports, discounts and advanced access to future books and courses. All for free. To learn more visit:

www.wjamesd.com/free-stuff

Holding Magnetic Conversations
Learn to Be a Master Communicator in Just Hours

First Edition (*sm*)

ISBN – 978-0-9915587-2-8 (ebk)
ISBN – 978-0-9915587-3-5 (sc)

Table of Contents

INTRODUCTION

Just like the right mindset which develops a good attitude and strong character, effective communication is a critical part of advancing through life. Understanding how to communicate your ideas and goals is an essential life and business skill. After all, where would we be as a society if we couldn't communicate with one another?

This manual builds off the information in my business book, <u>Unlocking the Small Business Game</u>. I'll be using terminology and pulling from concepts presented there but you do not have to read that book to benefit from this one.

To learn more please visit me at: **www.wjamesd.com**

All the information presented here is made to get two main things accomplished.

(1) To learn how to use communication to receive and give necessary information and

(2) To learn how communication is the foundation of having a "magnetic personality". Properly used, you can *magnetize* people to you; you want people to be drawn to you but we want them to *stick* around also. Magnets stick to metal and we need people to stick with us just a few minutes, sometimes for days, years or even life.

The two ideas above are effective in life and business. From talking with your loved ones, to business networking and on to speaking to your customers (or potential customers), this information is vital to success. Lack of communication is the cause of many problems. Effective communication is a priceless resource and improper communication limits opportunity.

This simple understanding of communication, what it is and its often untapped potential, will elevate whatever it is you're trying to do. Period, bottom line.

If it's true that the majority of our communication is idle and unfocused, then just the simple act of knowing how to steer a conversation can make a difference. Rest assured, almost everything I know about how to hold "magnetic conversations" is presented to you now.

Don't be fooled by the length of this book. We will be covering a lot of information in a short period of time. I purposely wrote the book this way so you could get to the skills and techniques you need quickly. Also, when you come back and reference them, you don't have to read anything that is not relevant.

If you're ready, then let's get to it.

Chapter 1 : THE SENSES & THE MIND

The secret to effective communication is a skill that eludes many. I mean really, who takes the time to effectively communicate with people? Many figure, "Hey! What's the point?" But in our society it's absolutely vital to understand that everything you want to do, everything you want to accomplish, must be done through other people at some point or another.

The lack of good communication is the key to a lot of our personal problems. It affects us in relationships, at our jobs, in the classrooms and in our society and culture in general.

Everybody's talking to one another, but it's *not* effective conversation!

Let's pause here a moment. Now, what do I mean by effective communication? Simply, it's a communication that allows all the people involved to have a chance to *bond*. This bonding has been referred to as chemistry or magnetism.

It's more than just words; it's about communicating with your whole body.

Body language counts as much as 80% or more of our total communication. Do you realize that most people (and you're probably guilty of this yourself), only pick up a little more than 70% of what you actually say? The other 30% of the time you're talking people are either thinking of what they will say next, or thinking of something else entirely. The mind is constantly wandering and will continue to do so unless it has a focus point.

So the first thing we need to learn in effective communication is to force the person's mind to give more of its attention to you. How is this done? By making use of the other person's senses – Occupying them so to speak. I'm sure you are familiar with the five senses.

Touch

Taste
Smell
Sight
Hearing

To occupy the mind, you must occupy the senses. The more senses you can occupy the more attention you'll get from that person.

Let's throw out the sense of taste. Occupying this sense is rather pointless for conversation.

The sense of touch is to be used with caution, so use it only as a greeting. It's very easy to hold out your hand and get a shake from just about anyone – Men, women and even most children. In Western culture, the hand shake is so ingrained in us we do it without even thinking.

Smell is easy. Be clean and always keep a nice smelling cologne or perfume on you. Use enough for people around you to smell, but never overdue it. An overwhelming scent, even a good one, is more of a distraction for the mind then it is an attention grabber.

Sight is another easy one. Always keep your appearance presentable. You don't have to look like you've stepped out of a glamour magazine, but you should look decent enough as to not turn people off. A note here, in the many sub-cultures of our society what's acceptable in terms of appearance varies from group to group. Be yourself, add in your personality to your style but never forget, people *do* judge books by their cover. This is a weakness of the human mind and it is a fact that you must learn to accept.

Also how you stand, walk and move your hands says a lot about your level of confidence (refer to, Unlocking the Small Business Game, Chapter Six).

The sense of Hearing is self explanatory. This guide is all about communication, isn't it?

So as you occupy the senses of the other person or people, you need to make sure that you don't overdo it. Meaning, it is quite possible that you look so spectacular (*hey, it's possible*) that the person looks more at how you're dressed then pay attention to what you're saying. This can happen and does happen a lot more than you may realize. Another instance that can happen is that you look like you're out of a person's "reach". They may see you as far above their "level". This has both positive and negative benefits depending on the situation you are in. The worst negative is that people separate themselves from you so much, that they feel they cannot relate to you. There may even be a small intimidation factor involved.

Always keep in mind that women are especially good at seeing details that men miss. They have their own filter and unique way of breaking apart appearances. Many psychologists agree that this has to do with a woman's natural survival instincts.

So how do we occupy senses over the phone and in written communication? Be patient we'll get to that soon. Now that we've gotten the boring stuff out of the way, let's dig in!

Chapter 2 : IT'S ALL ABOUT ENERGY

Now that you have the mind more focused in your direction it's time to pull them into your "world" by putting out energy. And by energy I mean enthusiasm and a general confidence in what you're saying.

A master Communicator realizes that he or she is on stage. Its lights, camera and action! You must develop the ability to pull people out of "their world" and into yours.

Pulling a person "into you world", is largely based on accepting the fact that people's moods effect their energy level.

How people think, affect how they feel and how they feel usually reflects in their body language and the way they communicate.

People sad or depressed usually walk with their shoulder slumped over. People upset or irritated usually keep a lot of tension in their face, particularly around their eyes. They also keep tension in their upper back and shoulder area. All of these postures are the results of what they are feeling. And what they are feeling is coming from what they're thinking.

To not only grab someone's attention, but hold it, you must not only occupy the senses, but your body language must reflect a person who is relaxed and easy going. This will bring a comfortable "vibe" into the situation.

Next you must give off your energy to them so that they become receptive. I said give off, not push it on them. If you push, most people will resist, especially if they're in a bad mood.

Now, how does this work?

Simple. Have you ever been around a depressed person? They are moping around and talking slow and in a low tone. Don't they seem to just suck energy out of the room?

Matter of fact, if you give in to that "vibe", you may start feeling down and out yourself. It's almost all in the mind.

On the other side of the coin, have you been around a person who is positive and upbeat? Their energy almost seems to rub off on you. They leave a positive impression with you even if you don't know them.

So let's get back to how we accomplish this.

(1) Enthusiasm
(2) Confidence

Now, when I say enthusiasm I'm not talking about being a super happy babbling idiot. Smiling heavily and laughing at jokes that aren't funny. This comes off as fake and honestly, people may find it difficult to take you seriously. This is *not* what we want.

What I'm talking about is having complete and total confidence in what you say and what you do with your body language.

In other words, your energy must be higher than the person or people you're talking to. You must bring that certain "vibe" into the situation.

People are naturally drawn to people with higher energy (enthusiasm mixed with confidence). People who are comfortable with themselves and seem to know what they are saying and what they're doing can bypass almost any person's mood. This is a natural human reaction and by nature, people will respond to it. It's ingrained in our very genetic make-up.

To get an idea of what I mean let's look at Oprah. She brings a certain positive "vibe" with her and it infects the lives of millions of people.

Look at your favorite music star. Look at the character you most admire in your favorite movie or television show. Nearly nine times out of 10, they are the ones who yield this almost overwhelming charm, enthusiasm and confidence. Comedians are a prime example of this type of energy. Whether they are funny to you or not, they bring a strong vibe when they perform on stage; they command your attention. They almost always have clever things to say and do. Their energy is given off naturally, and this creates the magnetism.

If you have confidence in your conversation and can communicate well, you will also develop an infectious charisma.

So what is confidence? Simply said, confidence is *not* trying. It is valuing yourself and being completely comfortable with who and what you are at any given moment.

When you are confident you are not thinking about what may go wrong or even what the results of the conversation may be. Lack of confidence causes you to stumble over your words, second guess your word choices and blocks the flow of energy that you are trying to give off. It is like bending a water hose while the water is running; you are slowly cutting off the flow. Lack of confidence or trying to appear confident sends out the energy of insecurity. This is a bend in the water hose.

Confidence is a skill and it can be developed with practice just like any other skill. What we are really doing by having a higher energy level than those we are speaking with is forcing their mind into a state of comparison. The average person will compare themselves not with people they feel are less than them, but to people who are doing better (or appear to be better) than them.

When you speak well, look well, act well and are completely comfortable with who you are, you will capture a person's attention and they will try to bring up their energy level to compensate (to match yours).

There is a saying that is thrown around online a lot and the interpretations of this saying means well, but a Hustler knows a different interpretation. What is this saying?

"Water seeks its own level."

In science this simply means that without any outside forces acting on water, the top level of water will even out. Think of a bowl, even if you pour water in from only a single side, all the water will level out evenly once the pouring stops. This isn't the best example, but just stay with me.

People interpret these phenomena as, "Birds of a feather flock together," or people seeking out other people of their own social class and mentality. Again, this interpretation is fine but to a Hustler it means, that the lower (energy level is this case) will attempt to compensate to balance out with the higher. Nature seeks balance, and as a part of nature, so do human beings.

You must define this enthusiasm and confidence level in yourself. Once you find it, learn to project it. Give it off and be careful not to push it on people. There is no reason to be fake about it. If you're comfortable with you, it should come naturally.

Chapter 3 : THE KEY TO MAGNETIC CONVERSATIONS

Here's a quick recap from, <u>Unlocking the Small Business Game,</u> on how to begin conversations. After this we'll get deeper into the subject.

The best and easiest way to bring people into your world, after you have successfully brought that "vibe" into the situation is get them into a conversation.

Remember, you can start a conversation on three main subjects:

(1) The person you're talking to
(2) Yourself
(3) The situation

To start a conversation with anyone you can make a comment or ask a question about any of the three subjects above. Asking a question is usually best. Remember it should be what's called an open-ended question.

An open-ended question is a question that cannot be answered with just a yes or no. You want to avoid questions that people can give one word answers to.

Use open-ended questions to force people to give you information. And knowing how and when to use this information is the heart and soul of Magnetic Conversation. A few examples:

What did you do today?

What's the best place to eat around here?

How do think this outfit looks on me?

How can we make our relationship better?

If you noticed, all these questions began with the words "what" or "how". There are eight basic ways to begin questions:

Who
What
When
Where
Why
How
So
Are (And Are)

Until you grow skilled in asking the right type of questions, it's much easier to stick with "what" and "how" in the beginning. Now, in order to pull information from someone, the question must be structured correctly.

If you don't get anything else from this book, you have to remember this. What I'm about to tell you is the missing ingredient in both influencing people and magnetizing people to you through conversation. If you fully understand what I'm about to tell you, I guarantee that not only will you look at conversations differently, but you'll become better at listening also. The better you listen, the more meaningful a conversation is to you. And when a person feels that you are giving them your undivided attention, they will in turn give you more of their attention. The lower will compensate to match the higher.

Are you ready? Here it is:

The person who asks the right kind of questions, controls the conversation.

Think about that for a moment.

Do you realize that you can find out almost anything you want to know about a person if you can magnetize them to you, and then ask the right kind of questions?

This knowledge is extremely powerful and for a good many reasons.

When you ask questions, not only do you control the topic and speed of the conversation, you also seem to show great interest in what the person is saying. This in turn keeps them magnetized to you.

Who doesn't want to talk to a person who is listening to them? Who doesn't want to talk to a person who is giving them (or appears to be giving them) their full, undivided attention? We all want to be heard. Are you with me so far?

With the right questions, you can literally hold an entire conversation with someone and only talk for about 30% of the conversation!

For those of you who are not social extroverts, this should turn on a light bulb for you.

Did you know that for most people, hearing the sound of their own name immediately breaks their train of thought and commands their attention? Part of the reason this is true is because people have a favorite subject and that subject is *them*! If you don't believe me then obviously you haven't been paying much attention to your social media news feed.

Now let's move on to what you do with all these answers you get from the questions you ask.

Chapter 4 : THE BALL – YOUR COURT OR MINE?

So now you've asked the person you're talking to an open-ended question. They have given you a response. Now it's your job to take what's in that response and do one of two things:

(1) Run with the ball (*do the talking yourself*)
(2) Or put the ball back in their court (*return their answer and ask a new question*)

Allow me to illustrate this:

You: How are you feeling today?

Person: Eh, I'm doing well, I guess.

<u>Pause here.</u> Now mentally we have to decide what we are going to do with this information. If we take the first route (running with the ball) your response might be something like this:

You: I'm doing great myself! I think today is going to be a pretty good day. If everything happens like I planned it, I'll be smiling ear to ear when I get home tonight.

See that? In this example, you took the information and built a response off of one **key-word** that they gave us. The word "good".

We **elevated** the word "good" to the word, "great". Why? Because our energy needs to be higher than theirs. Always give out your energy. And remember energy here means – Enthusiasm and Confidence.

If they say they're doing ok. You say you're doing good.

If they say they're doing good, you say you're doing great.

If they say they're doing great, you say you're doing outstanding.

Now let's look at your possible response if we, "put the ball back in their court".

You: Nice to see that you're doing good. What are you doing later on this evening?

In this example, instead of talking about ourselves from the information they gave us, we just took what they gave us and asked them another question. This of course forces them to continue to open up and give more information. When we get that information, we either run with it, or put in back in their court and the conversation continues back and forth like that.

So you may be thinking, which option should I use? Should I "run with the ball" or "put the ball back in their court"?

The answer is this:

Run with the ball when you want to:
(1) Make a point
(2) Tell a story
(3) Or relate to what they're saying to build rapport (giving off your energy)

Put the ball back in their court when you want to:
(1) Continue to dig for specific information
(2) Want them to tell a story
(3) Want them to reveal information about themselves or the topic

I know that may be a lot to swallow all at once. They don't teach this stuff in school so most of this may be foreign to you.

If I've lost you at any point here, please stop and reread it until you understand it.

Remember when you ask a question you must listen to their response. Out of this response you want to identify a **key-word**. This **key-word** gives you a basis for what to say next.

If you're running with the ball (doing the talking yourself), you **elevated** the **key-word**. And if you put the ball back in their court (return the answer) you use the **key-word** in your response to let them know that you're listening and then you ask a new question.

If possible, this new question should be based off of the **key-word** you've chosen. This won't always be a possibility, but if you can then go for it.

One more set of examples before we continue.

Running With the Ball
You: What happened last night?

Person: What didn't happen? (*Laughs*) I almost got into a car accident. Damn drunk almost hit me coming home from the bar.

You: (*Grabbing the **key-word** accident*) Wow! Are you serious? I couldn't even imagine being in an accident, especially if I'm out just having a good time. I mean that would just completely devastate your whole night! (*You gave a little information then **elevated** on the accident to make it sound more serious than what it was*)

Putting the Ball Back in Their Court
You: What happened last night?

Person: What didn't happen? (*Laughs*) I almost got into a car accident. Damn drunk almost hit me coming home from the bar.

You: (*Grabbing the **key-word** accident*) Wow! That's serious right there. If you were in an accident last night how do you think Sheryl would have handled it? (*You make a comment and then ask another question based on the **key-word** you've chosen*)

There is no right or wrong way to grab **key-words**. In these examples you could have easily grabbed the word "drunk" or even "bar". The **key-word** you choose is not what's important. What's important is the fact that you properly respond in one of the two ways mentioned above.

This takes practice to develop the skill, but when you do, you can literally create entire conversations off of nearly any topic under the sun.

Above all, please remember not to just ask anything but question after question. You are not holding a job interview! Relax a bit and throw in some information too. We'll get more into that in Chapter Six.

Chapter 5 : THE ART OF PICTURES & STORYTELLING

Human beings since recorded time have always learned best in pictures, images and stories. The biggest reason being is that we naturally think in picture and/or image forms. Not words.

Quick example. If I say the word elephant, what comes to mind?

The actual word *elephant*? No! An image of an elephant pops into your head.

How about the words *fire* or *car* or *home*? All mental pictures, correct?

Even abstract concepts are broken down as pictures. How about the word *love*? What symbol represents that? A heart.

Here's an interesting one, how about the word *stereotype*? What images come up there? A few I'm sure.

Here's the key. Every noun and pronoun in the English language (and in almost all languages) brings pictures and/or images to our mind.

This is also true of some verbs such as the word *hate*, and many adjectives such as the word *running*. Can you see the potential in knowing this when communicating with others?

By constantly "sprinkling" your conversation with nouns and pronouns (we'll stick with these two just to keep things simple), you can further keep the mind magnetized on you.

The mind of the person you're talking to will not only picture and imagine what you're saying, but they will also "feel" it on an emotional level. Why? Because we all have feelings associated with pictures and images.

As you're speaking with people, asking questions and making comments, it's important every now and then to relate to something that the person is saying.

The best way to do this is by telling a story. If you're not a good story teller (like myself), it doesn't matter. All you have to do is make sure as you tell your story that you add in those nouns and pronouns. Make them "feel" and picture what you're saying.

Don't just say, "I went to the store yesterday." Try, "On my way to the store yesterday I was listening to that new radio station and they played some excellent (*give the energy*) music!"

Don't just say, "I can't believe my son got suspended for fighting yesterday."

Try, "I am so pissed (*give the energy*)! Can you believe that hard-headed son of mine got into a fight at school yesterday? Not only that, he got suspended. We sat down and had a long, serious conversation after that. I told him that the next time he has an issue that huge with a classmate to tell his teacher and to let me know. Next time I hope he thinks first before something like that happens again. What would you do in a situation like that?

Did you catch the open-ended question at the end of that last example? Guess what? You just told a story (as short as it was) and went right back into involving the other person into the conversation. Pretty easy, isn't it?

It's the back and forth exchange of energy, directed by your enthusiasm, confidence and questions that creates and maintains magnetism.

The power of the story (properly told) is powerful. Do you realize that almost everything is a story? Books, movies, television shows, even commercials (the good ones) tell a 30 second story.

To further prove my point, take the following scene.

Michael woke up sick. He grabbed a Kleenex in the box on his night stand and blew his nose.

Simple and boring – there is nothing there that exuded any energy, enthusiasm, or feeling. Now let's look at the scene again.

Michael woke up. The sun's rays cut through the blinds from his bedroom window. The light was clear, bright and painful to his eyes. He was sweaty and hot. His body ached as he reached over to his night stand and snatched a Kleenex from the box. Michael blew his nose forcibly into the thin sheet.

Although the second example is slightly exaggerated, you can pick up on the fact that Michael is sick without the word "sick" ever being mentioned. The way the scene is described brings out memories from you because you have felt this way at some point in your life. When you felt this way you more than likely had a cold and a fever. You emotionally respond to the scene because you can "feel" what Michael is feeling.

Take this knowledge and use it in your communications. This is especially effective in writing. Bring them from their world into yours and hold them there.

Chapter 6 : MAKE LESS COMMENTS, MAKE MORE OBSERVATIONS

Here another small technique to further enhance your communication skills.

Now most of the time, we tend to strangle the life out of a conversation simply by the way we answer questions and make comments.

I have already taught you to ask open-ended questions to elicit more information from the person you're speaking with, but you have to do the same in order to keep the conversation flowing and interesting.

If someone tells you that they want to go back to school for example, don't leave them with a closed comment.

Here's what I mean:

Person: You know, I've been thinking, I should go back to school.

You: I think that's a good idea.

This type of comment gives nothing to the conversation and if the other person isn't what you'd call a "conversationalist", this may very well be the beginning and end of the topic and possibly the conversation itself.

You must learn to stop making comments and give out that energy in the form of observations.

Let's look at this again.

Person: You know, I've been thinking, I should go back to school.

You: That's going to be a challenge with you working full-time and still making time for your family, but I know it's for the best. When you finally finish there's no telling where you can go. Oh and think of all that money you will be making! So, (*one of the eight ways to begin an open-ended question*) what do you plan on going back to school for?

Do you see the difference? An observation lets the person know you're listening to them and that you have an interest in the topic. This subtle difference plays right back into what we've just talked about. The back and forth exchange between the person and yourself.

You ask them to reveal some information and they do. You make an observation about what they say and then "run with the ball" or "put the ball back in their court" to get even more information.

Another example:

You: What's your plan for the weekend?

Person: Not quite sure yet. If it's nice out, I think I might open up the grill and throw on some steaks.

You: Nice! I haven't had a good steak in a long time. I'm not too bad on the grill myself. It takes real skill to get those steaks sizzling just right. I think a big secret to great flavor is the right kind of charcoal. What kind of charcoal do you use?

Again, this takes a little practice but once you get it you'll wonder why you've communicated any other way.

When making observations it's ok to give your opinion, but if you can bring in facts about the topic, this is even more powerful.

If the person who you're speaking with happens to drop some facts your way that you can't deny are true, then pay them a compliment on their knowledge and/or expertise.

People love to be thought of as intelligent and insightful. If they are, then by all means let them know it!

Chapter 7 : OVER THE PHONE, ONLINE AND IN PRINT

At the beginning we talked about how to occupy the senses of the person you're talking to. The question is how do you do that if you're over the phone or communicating in an online forum for example?

This may sound strange, but a person naturally concentrates more on a conversation when they are talking over the phone. Thousands of cell phone related car accidents a year can't be wrong. And texting accidents beat verbal accidents hands down.

Think about it like this. When a person is over the phone you are occupying their sense of hearing. Your presence in this way is magnified by the simple fact that your voice is literally *in* their ear.

This is a strange quirk in human behavior but can be easily used to your advantage. All you have to do is keep up a good, magnetic conversation. There will always be a few distractions on their end and on yours, but if the conversation is good, they will focus on it.

Now when you're online you only occupy one of their senses that of course is sight. If you are in a chat room, the sense of touch is also occupied.

The key here is short sentences using a lot of nouns and pronouns to continually keep images and pictures in their mind.

If your response or observation is rather long, write only a sentence or two per line. Post those and then continue for another sentence or two then post those. This draws their eyes down and helps to hold their attention while they piece together your entire post; everything you're trying to say.

This is not only easier on the eyes to read, but it's also gives you time to think about proper sentence structure. And I'm not talking English class structure here either. What I mean is talking about Magnetic

Conversation structure; nouns, pronouns and clever observations about the current topic. Add in some compelling questions and interesting observations and you can magnetize them just as easily as if you were face to face.

The point I want you to get here is that even when you are at a disadvantage at getting their attention, you can still magnetize them with careful wording and questions.

You are never too far away to make impressions in people's minds. If you can master the verbal skills, you can even translate this into writing! Good columnists and authors do it all the time. You have to literally imagine you're talking to someone while you write.

Think of questions that may come up and answer them. Make carefully worded observations and flow from one idea or concept to the next. Lead the conversation with questions, and they will follow.

Ask simple questions (open-ended of course) that have common answers. When you respond to them in your writing, people will agree with you and are forced to accept what you're talking about.

In writing (just like in selling) if you can get people to agree with on point after point after point, when you get to the real point you're trying to make, they are more likely to see your side.

They may not agree, but they won't knock what you've said. After all, they've agreed with all your other points.

Written communication is often the hardest to master because you have no immediate feedback and are forced to create your own. By keeping written communication simple and making general observations that most people can relate to, you can predict what the response may be, and continue writing as if you actually received a response. Be careful to never ramble on about just yourself when writing, you want to engage the reader by asking questions as well.

Again, if you master the verbal communication, written communication will become very easy.

Chapter 8 : WHAT TO DO WHEN THINGS GO BAD

Sometimes no matter how much energy we give out and how well we are using Magnetic Conversation skills, the other person is not giving us enough information to build off of.

This can be terrible especially if you're speaking with a potential business client or trying to *woo* that special someone you've had your eye on.

When this happens don't tense up and don't stop giving out your energy (unless they're just overly negative, then my advice is just get away from them).

What you do in this situation is simply reverse roles.

This simply means that instead of leading the conversation (with questions); flip it around so they lead the conversation. How do you do this? Simply get them to start asking questions. Put them in a position that they must ask you questions if they want the conversation to advance.

It's as simple as saying something like:

"You know, I feel like taking up the whole conversation. Tell me what what's on your mind. I'm just curious."

This line, or something similar to it, puts complete control of the conversation in their hands. Usually they will respond with a topic and you take that topic, make an observation and then give it back to them with an open-ended question asking them what they think about it.

Be careful here, getting people to open up who are shy, or simply don't want to, requires you to slow down the pace of the conversation.

The pace you slow it down to, is the pace *they* set.

Another way to do this is when they respond with what's on their mind, you just say, "Interesting, go on." This allows them open up at their own pace.

The worst thing that can happen here is that they say nothing is on their mind. Or they just shrug and close up. So this is when you pull the big guns out.

You simply shut-up and sit there in silence. That's right, silence. This applies a very uncomfortable pressure to the situation.

Just remember that pressure bursts pipes. If you can remain in silence long enough, they will eventually "burst" and attempt to start the conversation back up. A very sneaky tactic, but none the less very effective.

The magnetism you are trying to generate works best in people who are receptive to it. If they're not in the beginning, and they feel that you know that, they will usually open up for you. All you have to do is give them the opportunity. It's amazing how long five or 10 seconds in silence can be.

If they have no interest in starting the conversation back up then they'll find a way to make their exit.

Don't look at this as a failure; just simply understand that you can't win them all. Forcing conversation is a lot more embarrassing then staying silent for a moment or two. If you've ever tried to force a conversation to happen, then you know what I'm talking about here.

Sometimes, regardless of what you do, things between you and the person you're talking to just won't "click". When this happens, don't worry and don't start to play yourself down to please them. Do not drop your energy level to theirs. Remember, being comfortable, even in silence or at the risk of failure exudes confidence.

If you're in a business situation where you are trying to Network with a fellow entrepreneur or possibly "hook" that big client, realize that if things aren't going well to stay committed to the reason you're there.

People are more likely to do business with people they like. Even if the conversation isn't going well they will respect you a lot more if you continue to just be yourself than if you try to "play up" to them.

Most people can sense an ass-kisser a mile away and if that's what they want out of you, then that just may be an indication that perhaps they aren't a future client you need to do business with anyway.

Opportunities are abundant if you keep an eye out for them. Again, you can't win them all.

Chapter 9 : COLOR AND CONTRAST

Imagine your favorite movie for a moment. Think about the character you most identify with. Next think about your favorite scene in that movie.

Now imagine having to watch that same exact scene over and over again. I'm talking back to back. Same dialogue or action, same setting and the same situation happening repeatedly for hours.

After a few times I'm sure you'll get pretty bored and lose interest. Unfortunately many of us do the same thing in a conversation.

If I repeated the word "run" over and over again, how long do you think I would hold your interest?

Run

Run

Run

Run

Run

That's just boring enough to read let alone say to someone, don't you agree? Now if I repeated the word "fast" over and over again, eventually the same thing would happen. Boredom and a loss of interest.

Fast

Fast

Fast

Fast

Fast

Now let's put them together.

Run fast

Fast run

Run fast

Fast run

Run fast

Still nothing great about it, but it holds your attention a little longer, doesn't it?

It's this contrast in the way words and sentences are used and grouped together that's helps hold people's attention.

Let's go back to your favorite movie and your favorite character. Chances are, in that movie, the character went through ups and downs, faced some challenges and hardships and eventually came to a new level of understanding about something or themselves, am I right?

Again it goes back to the story. And how does this story play out? It plays out in contrast.

The character begins the movie one way and by the end they become something different. During that whole time in between lies the heart and soul of the story. Every scene leads to a different scene without each scene repeating.

How does this translate to communication?

Simply reveal different things about yourself. When you make observations and tell stories mix things up in the process.

Don't just tell how you felt and what you thought about what happened. But also tell how the person you were in the situation with thought and reacted as well.

Don't go and on about the same topic. Cleverly ask your open-ended questions to change the topic of discussion before it gets boring or repetitive.

Remember – **The person asking the right kind of questions controls the conversation.**

Create that contrast in your communication. Move smoothly from topic to topic, tell interesting stories and make observations.

It's like two people dancing together. There's always the leader but each person can work off of one another's actions and reactions. At some point, they almost seem to move in sync with one another. All movements are on time and work well together.

Now we will close this book with the "magic ingredient" that is the essence of Magnetic Conversations and bring this all together.

Chapter 10: TONALITY

As we've already covered, the majority of communication has very little to do with exact words you use. How you *say* the words you use on the other hand is extremely important.

Say the word, "Hello," out loud in your normal speaking voice. Notice the plainness of your tone.

Now say the word again but drop your tone at the end of the word. Make the last two letters, "l-o" very low.

Now you probably feel silly and anyone who heard that would look at you as if you had some mental issues. But look at the effect, same word, entirely different *feeling*.

Now raise your voice slightly on the last two letters, the "l" and the "o". Don't raise the volume of your voice, just the tone. Smile as the last letters roll off of your tongue.

The word should feel warmer and more inviting. If not, try it again and pay attention to your voice's inflection and tone.

Now say the word, "Stop," in your plain speaking voice. Then say it again forcibly, as if you were trying to prevent a child from touching a hot stove. Notice the authority of that tone. This word became not just a word, but a command just by the change of tone.

Now, what changes the tones of the words you use? Simple. The **intention** behind them.

Say this sentence out loud in a normal speaking voice.

"We're going out for dinner tonight, right?"

Plain, boring. No energy, no enthusiasm and no confidence. Now say the sentence again, but this time as you say the word, "right," raise the tone. The intention behind the word should be that of agreement. If you say this correctly, your eyebrows should raise.

You want to convey the message, "You better agree," *without* saying it. It must come across with only your tone. What you're really saying is this:

"You *know* we're going out for dinner tonight."

But the first sentence, formed as a question in the right tone, is less blunt and just as effective and in some cases even more effective. Why? Because you gave the illusion of choice.

Quick changes in tone are very effective when forcing someone to zero in and listen to you. Say the following sentence in your plain speaking voice:

"Hello, Michael. Do you mind coming over here a moment? I have something important to tell you."

We have three sentences and now we will give each its own tone.

First we say, "Hello," and will raise our tone on the letters "l-o" like we did before. This commands attention and piques interest. Don't forget to smile with it.

In our next sentence we will hold the **intention** of urgency. Say this sentence as if what you have to say is the most important thing Michael can hear at this moment in his life.

Practice it a few times. If you listen carefully you can hear the correct tone when you finally hit it. The emphasis in this sentence should be on the words, "mind" and "coming".

If you are having trouble squint your eyes as you say it. You read that correctly. Squint your eyes as you say the second sentence to help bring the tone of urgency across.

Now in the last sentence, we will drop our tone. Not drop it to an inaudible whisper, but low enough to make it appear as if this is a secret.

Whenever you say anything with the intention of *secrecy* or *mystery* behind it, the tone and volume of your voice will naturally drop. Try it a few times. Once again, you will feel when you get it right.

When you feel comfortable, put all three sentences together. Pique interest by raising your tone in the greeting. Create urgency by conveying seriousness in the second sentence and finally draw Michael in by creating mystery and secrecy in the final sentence.

You just used three different tones to create three different emotional responses in Michael.

Simple, wasn't it?

As you grow more skilled with your communication, begin to pay attention to the tones you use. Proper tonality can command attention, demand authority, captivate, empower and influence. Just study your favorite actor or comedian. Instead of watching them, close your eyes and just listen to their tones as they deliver their lines. I guarantee you that you will hear them as you've never heard them before.

Once you develop these skills, they will become second nature. You won't even have to think about them.

The techniques used in, <u>Holding Magnetic Conversations</u>, are a skill worth your time to develop. It will help you go from point A to point B then on to point C, etc. in all your relationships.

Please don't doubt the simplicity of this material. It's my job to keep things easy and comprehensive. Make the effort and just do it. You'll be amazed at the results.

As it was once told to me, "It's a vibe. You just have to catch it."

Thanks for your time and interest in this material. I toast to your continued advancement in all areas of your life.

About the Author

W. James Dennis started his first business when he was 17 years old. It failed. He then started his second business in his early-twenties, which failed too. But just a few years later with an example of business success to learn from, his third business did succeed and he operated it for over 10 years. During this time he was a dedicated student of the "Game", something which he calls, *Uncommon Sense*. Realizing his passion was writing and educating, he changed gears in his life and is now an author, public speaker and small business consultant living just outside of Atlanta, Georgia – United States. His favorite quote is, "Keep it moving and keep it simple in the process."

Connect with W. James Dennis

www.wjamesd.com
wjamesdennis@gmail.com
facebook.com/wjamesd
twitter: @wjamesdennis

Also by This Author

Unlocking the Small Business Game – *The Playbook for Starting a Small Business from Nothing Using Simple Clear Uncommon Sense*

Revealing the Secrets of the Game – *Exposing the Most Heavily Guarded System of Self-Empowerment Ever Designed*

QUICK NOTES

- Always occupy the senses to give the mind a focal point
- Always give out more energy (enthusiasm and confidence) than the person (or people) you are speaking to

- **The 3 subjects used to start a conversation:**
(1) The person
(2) Yourself
(3) The situation

- **The 8 open-ended question starters:**
(1) Who
(2) What
(3) When
(4) Where
(5) Why
(6) How
(7) So
(8) Are (And Are)

- **What to do with a response from a person:**
(1) Run with the ball
(2) Put the ball back in their court

- Use **key-words** as a basis to what to say next
- Use nouns and pronouns to help create mental images and tell stories
- Make fewer comments and make more observations
- Increase a person's attention by using contrasting examples, stories and observations
- Don't forget to use tonality to maximize the power and impact of words and sentences

Made in United States
Troutdale, OR
10/31/2024

24266801R00022